SAY GOODBYE:
you may never see them again

Scenes from two East-End backgrou
Paintings · John Allin   Text · Arnold Wesker

Jonathan Cape Thirty Bedford Square London

First published 1974
Reissued in paperback 1983
Text © 1974 by Arnold Wesker
Paintings © 1974 by John Allin
Jonathan Cape Ltd, 30 Bedford Square, London WC1

ISBN 0 224 02965 7

Printed in Italy by Amilcare Pizzi, Milano

The paintings by John Allin are reproduced by courtesy of
the Portal Gallery Ltd, London W1 who are the sole
representatives for the artist's work.

Arnold Wesker
'… It's a trap, the East End, to be sentimental and
full of cosy longing for "the good old days" … I
mean, *I* may have loved it … written about it with
love, but my family remember it with misery. *I* may
be riddled with nostalgia, hoarding the past as
though it were food for a time of famine, but
not them, not them … Nothing good about "the
good old days" for them … Being romantic, yes!
That's looking back with love, no one minds that,
but sentimentality? That's looking back with
dishonesty …'

Collection : Neville Smith

To My Wife and Daughter: Phyllis and Sharon

with love   *John*

To My aunts: Ann Betty Billie Esther Lily Rae and Ray and Sara

My uncles: Barney Harry and Harry Perly Sammy and Solly

My cousins: Annie Belle Bert Billie Bryan David Doris Freyda June Lily Maurice Monty Nita Norma Rachel Ralph Sid Shifra Thelma Tom (all being merely the English contingent)

With love   *Arnold*

John Allin
'Can't you sentimentalize the East End by always *making it slummy, though? I mean,* my *mother also hated it, but I saw it as a place where people lived, earned their living, grew up, moved on ... they had dignity ... I like painting the past with dignity ...'*

'...Fashion Street...Weaver Street...The Old-Lady-of-Thread-a-Needle Street...names! I love them!..."Mum! throw me down a penny!" I used to stand across the road in Fashion Street where we lived and call up "throw me down a penny!" and down it would come, odd coppers, screwed up in a piece of paper...Fournier Street... Charlotte de Rothschild's Dwellings...Itchy Park ...Old Jewry...Huguenots, Irish, Jews, tramps...

'... tramps! Annie Wobbler—*she* was a tramp. Used to "do" for us in Fashion Street. There we were, an attic with two rooms and a gas-stove on the landing, and we had this "help" who called my parents "the madam" and "the master" and me and my sister "little mistress" and "little master" ... We used to invent her past, thought she'd once been a maid for aristocracy ... Poor Annie! She was a bit mental by the time she reached us. Wore a mass of skirts and petticoats with all manner of things hidden in them: tin mug, cutlery, paper bags ... very haughty she was. I mean—what was there to keep clean in Fashion Street? Stone stairs? Some squares of linoleum? She'd scrub the stone stairs, maybe the floors ... an excuse, really, for my mother to give her some coppers and a mug of tea and bread and butter. Annie Wobbler! Spoke "refained" ... slept in Itchy Park, with the other tramps ...'

Collection: Della and Ralph Saltiel

Collection : Tom Maschler

'… My grandfather was hard as nails … Here, know what he used to do? His favourite trick? Used to come into the house where we lived in Churchill Walk and throw a couple of bars of chocolate and two cubes of Oxo on the table. The chocolate was to share out among nine kids and the Oxo was to go with the meal. What meal, though? My gran knew what meal. She knew what that Oxo meant—a trip to the workhouse for meal-tickets! My mother says that first of all grandad had to go and sign on on the Parish relief and then the family all had to troop over to the workhouse where, if they thought you was a deserving case, they'd dish you out with a coal-ticket worth about 1/6d which'd get you about half a hundredweight, a meat-ticket worth about 1/8d, and then in the workhouse itself she'd pick up four little packets of rice, sugar, tea and cocoa, you know? and two loaves of bread. The old men in the workhouse used to bake the bread, the old men on the dole … Once a week she could do that. And when she had all that she and my mum'd go down to the Salvation Army in Congress Hall on the Lower Clapton Road and get 2/6d each for a bit of scrubbing … In 1925 that was … Churchill Walk, quarter of a mile from Hackney Hospital, where I was born …'

'… My father was in and out of Hackney Hospital … dying …'

'… My step-father died there … cancer. Both my fathers died of cancer—Lung cancer, both of them! So my mother, she went through the whole ordeal twice … you know … ?'

'… Our poor mothers … the men always seemed to get struck down first, didn't they? The same with my mum, she had to nurse my father, same with her … three strokes he had, over fifteen years, and with each stroke he could do less and less … Tough old ladies, eh? All that generation were, though … What'll we be like, I wonder? …'

'…Flower and Dean Street…Whitechapel Road…Black Lion Yard…Where's the white chapel now? Bombed! And who ever owned black lions? And who *was* the old lady of Thread-a-needle Street…Yellow streets they were, foggy—do you know, I don't think I can remember summer in them, no! Strange, isn't it? They were such narrow streets, I suppose. I suppose there was so little sky could get through…But I remember gas lamps, and a man with a bike going round with a long pole with a hook on the end of it which he'd fit into a ring at the bottom of a chain and pull…and queueing of an evening for salt-beef sandwiches in Blooms…tight, close streets…Once I was left in the care of my sister and her friend and they went out for a minute, only a minute—and whoosh! out! out into the streets! Dressed, quick, and round the corner to my friends in Flower and Dean Street. Lost! *That* was an evening of panic…Flower and Dean Street…Wentworth Street…Old Montague Street…Thrawl Street! What did they mean? Thrawl Street! Who named them?'

Collection: Mr and Mrs R. P. Eaton

'...Pesha Chaia...Rocha...Bathsheba...exotic names! I drove my family silly forcing them to remember so's I could make a family tree ... Freyda ...Mendel...Basha...Modcha. But their children's names weren't so exotic: Rae, Sara, Annie, Billie—they were my aunts, my father's beautiful sisters ... Then there was my mother's side; her father used to be a Shoichet, a religious man, killed the animals in a special way; and her grandfather, also a religious man, used to write out the scripts when they'd faded, you know, those scrolls they keep in the ark, well they used to fade or crack from unrolling and rolling up ... Jacob ... Bella Toba ... Fatah Henchel ... Blimah ... who had Sarah, Ida, Bernard, Isadore, Minko, Oscar, Layosh, Osha, Herman, Ignatz, *and* Cecile Leah my mother ... they used to call my mother the little spitfire. Still is. *She* kept the family together, not my father—everyone just loved him ... Little thing my mother is, not much over four feet high, and all the children in the family measured themselves alongside her—at seven you were taller than her, see? ... even my kids did it: "Ooh look! we're nearly as tall as grandma!" ... On my father's side they came from the Ukraine, Dneiperpetrovsk. Lovely name isn't it? Dneiperpetrovsk! Katerinaslav ... names! Mendel, that was my grandfather's name, he ...

Collection : Norma and Mike Fisher

'…he was a very learned man, steeped in the Talmud, so the aunts told me. "And", my aunt Sara used to say, "I'll have you know your grandfather was one of the founder members of a tailors' trade union in Dneiperpetrovsk!' … He was blind, used to tap his way from Flower and Dean Street along Brick Lane one block to Fashion Street, came to eat Matzo Brile—matzos soaked in egg and fried, my children love it … But Rocha, the "boba", she was bed-ridden. I can always remember that she kept a purse under her pillow, full of farthings … When she died I tried to make my aunts laugh, I was about seven at the time, of course I couldn't. "People need time to grieve," they said … Rocha … Mendel … I loved them *and* their names … "Say Gyergyoszentmiklos," my mother used to tease me, that's where *she* was born, Transylvania, "say Harumcurt, Deva, Gyergoyszentmiklos… there was forests and high mountains and water-falls," she'd tell us, "and when we left Tran-sylvania a peasant, one of the neighbours, came and played a violin to us…"'

'...And Joe, my father...always out of work he was, preferred reading books...used to persuade me to play truant and go to pictures with him...He once went to the Jewish Board of Guardians for help—hard lot they were—they made him stand all the time while they asked him questions, and still they didn't give him any relief. Not, mind you, that my father was one to inspire confidence about the future. He hated tailoring and tailoring factories and tailoring types, and you could see it on his face, couldn't hide it! Despised it!...give him a good dis-cussion! Loved talking with people...So, my mother had to drive him as well as herself...I once had to sell my stamp collection so's to have money for the week. Got £2.10s for it...Gave me a great pleasure to do that...wasn't a very good collection anyway. The best things in it were some huge coloured Russian stamps which my aunt Sara brought back from a trip there. She was a trade union leader—one of the first of the "women", tiny—and a talker? Indomitable! Treasurer for the London branch of the garment workers' union she was...And I remember, every Sunday morning till quarter to one on the dot, my father used to stand around on the Whitechapel Road, by Black Lion Yard, with all the other Jewish tailors, waiting for a guv'nor to come up and offer him a job—if he needed it—arguing politics with his cronies...the "chazar mark" it was called, the "pig market", I sometimes stood around with him...you can still see them there, standing around, waiting, arguing politics...no kids with them now, though...'

Collection: Cecil Gee International

Collection : Tom Maschler

'…Charlotte de Rothschild's Dwellings! Posh sounding isn't it? And what were they? Tenements! With no bathrooms, no hot water and poky space … but it was interesting, really, because these flats all centred round a playground where I spent a lot of time playing, and when you were in it it looked like Sing-Sing prison, but—no traffic! A private space! Surrounded by family, closed-in, protected … not of course your flowered enclosures, but still, a private space. Privacy, for working-class families, in those days!

'…Kids!…Warm, sunny days…doing all the things kids did when they played in the street. Having seasons. One of conkers, one of bows-and-arrows, one of building your own scooter with ball-bearing wheels, you know? Everything that cost nothing, you did!— that cost your parents nothing, you did to "amuse" yourself. Bicycle wheels, using them as hoops, remember that? And marbles, cigarette-cards, flicking them up against the wall, and pitch and toss, with halfpennies? You had the seasons and they came round. Every year! Industriously on the same time. Like some people go to Ascot … idyllic days. And romantic. They were romantic … entertaining yourself, being inventive …'

'Churchill Walk…de Beauvoir Road…pre-war days…Saturday summer evenings walking the dog round de Beauvoir Square…the doors were always open. Mrs Stocker next door would come to the top of the stairs and—this is it, word for word: "Coo-ooh!" she'd go at the top of my grandmother's stairs, who incidentally lived in the basement. "You there, Rose?" "Ere, come down, Lil." "Got a couple of pounds of sugar?"…Right? Got it? Away!… And she'd do likewise to Mrs Stocker, you know? My first childhood memories were there. I lived in de Beauvoir Road till I was eleven but my Gran lived in Churchill Walk and I used to play there. My mum'd go out to work and then come and pick me up of an evening … and the fondest place in Churchill Walk was my grandmother's kitchen because there was always people popping in and out, talking, this that and the other. And there was always cousins … Because in Churchill Walk this was the situation, for years the situation was this: my uncle George, that was my mother's step-brother, right?

lived at number 18 Churchill Walk. My aunty Rosie, that was my mother's step-sister, one of her step-sisters, right? lived upstairs in 11 Churchill Walk. My uncle Ken moved from 11 Churchill Walk to number 4 Churchill Walk. When my father died, my first father, my mother moved to 4 Churchill Walk, upstairs, on the top floor, very much like your situation in Fashion Street. Right? My aunt Eileen came and lived on the middle floor of 4 Churchill Walk. My aunt Rosie and uncle Bill then moved from 11 Churchill Walk to number 5 Churchill Walk. My cousin Helen, who was my grandmother's sister's daughter, my aunt Nell's daughter, moved to 11 Churchill Walk and lived upstairs in the top flat where my aunt Rosie lived. My aunt Olive at one time lived in Churchill Walk, upstairs, always upstairs, even me and Phyllis lived in Churchill Walk when we first got married, upstairs, in number 11, my grandmother's house. So there it was! The whole cycle! For donkeys years—all contained with Browns and tentacles off the Brown family . . . Happy days, family around, you know? . . .'

Collection : Mr Arnold Bulka

' … But for me it was the pictures. If you had 6d it was swimming but if you had 1/– it was the "pitchers". "Please, mister, can you take me in?" Unless it was two U's and then you'd get in yourself … In them days there was 1/– in the front, 1/6 or 1/9 in the rear and about 2/– upstairs … And what you had was a commissionaire, his name was George, and he used to dress up. A real bruiser he was. Used to say he was an ex-professional boxer. And it was his delight to catch you bunking in. Used to pit his wits against yours. Over the years we twigged how to do it … wait till the end of a film, people'd come out and before the doors'd slam to you'd creep in and kick the door to make it sound as though they'd closed. Then …'

'...we used to get behind the red curtain and crawl along on our bellies to the front seats, not our hands and knees, he'd see us then, but Indian-like, on our bellies. And then we'd slither up to take our place on the front row. That'd be the hardest part. If he caught you then—you'd had it! If he missed—you'd get to see the film ...'

'It was the cinema for me also ... I'd nag and nag and nag to be taken ... unless there were gatherings. I remember, as a child, vividly, a flat filled with friends ... marvellous gatherings ... those little rooms in Fashion Street ... discussions ... gramophone recitals ... day hikes to Epping Forest and Box Hill ... I used to love the atmosphere, people coming and going ... You weren't only the child of your parents, you were the child of everyone because everyone took you out, gave you a penny, wagged their finger and gave you advice ...'

'Advice! My father was full of advice—about haircuts! A haircut was my idea of hell but my father was a fanatic about having them. Used to go prodigiously, without fail, every Saturday morning. He'd earn £2.10s as a foreman metal blender and he'd give my mum £2 and keep 10/- in his pocket for the week. And every Saturday, without fail, he used to go to Sidney Gershon's, the barber, lovely name isn't? Short back and sides. Felt undressed if he never had it done. Used to have that and a shave. But as a kid I hated haircuts. Hated them! 'Cos it was all cold afterwards and invariably you'd get the other kids laughing at you. A twopenny all-off! "Look," he'd say, "you've got a bloody bird's tail," and I'd have to go and have a twopenny all-off, sitting on this plank of wood which they'd have specially for small boys, the men all talking about football or work ... warm really ... like the whole area ... but I suppose—Oh! all those years look warm and sunny now. Except ... the rotten lousy war years when no one could be really happy ...'

Collection: Mr Russell Harty

'...*We was evacuated with my mother at the beginning of the war, me sister and meself, to a place called Marton. It was in the flat country, by Wisbech, that area, you know? Fen country ... and I remember distinctively, distinctively! getting on a train at Liverpool Street Station. Thousands of kids and their mothers, with gas masks. A complete adventure ...*'

'That's *exactly* what *I* remember. But I went with my sister's school, Spitalfields' Foundation, and— that's right!—we also went to the Fen country. I'm just remembering. We went to Ely. Adelaide and Ely! That's right! I remember those days ... On the station with gas masks ... and someone said to my mother, "Say goodbye, you may never see them again!" ...'

'*Right! I remember that. It was the school-teachers. Callous bitches! ...*'

'... And do you remember those, those ... steel combs, with teeth ...'

'*Nit combs!*'

'Nit combs! With teeth on each side. Nit combs! And we had our hair gone through ... kids with gas masks hanging round them ... in cardboard boxes ...'

'*Right! Little cardboard boxes ...*'

'... cardboard boxes with string, and a hole into which you put the nozzle of the mask ...'

'*... like an easter egg!*'

'Like an easter egg!'

'*Amazing!*'

'That was our first time in the country, wasn't it?'

'*Well, virtually ...*'

'Oh yes, of course! You went hop-picking didn't you? When we moved to Weald Square in Upper Clapton we had neighbours who did that ...'

'*But hop-picking was different. That was, that was ...*'

'... it was still the country ...'

'*Yes, it was the country but it was—fantastic! You know? A beautiful experience, something I'm glad I lived through, that experience. And it was romantic! I'm glad it was romantic! Bloody overjoyed it was romantic, you know? ... Looking back on it ...*'

'... But then early on, in the panic days, my sister left school and left me in Ely. Wanted to contribute to the war effort and work in munitions. And there was a farewell picnic on a river bank, and *I* cried and *she* cried ... and I kept writing, nagging to come back ... came back for the worst of the blitz ...'

'... *Everyone else's shelter was on top, Anderson shelters they were called, but this grandfather of mine, this master-builder, he went mad and buried ours! And on top he put rubble, big mounds of earth. Well, this particular night there was a terrible raid, like all hell let loose. Next morning, when we all come out, four houses completely gone! ...*
Funny old times ... my mother looks back on the war as nothing but being one hell. But then she was an adult—for us it was all romantic ... Here! remember sitting in them shelters and listening to them bombs?

'... I remember always wanting to come up and look at the flack and the stars ...'

'... *and being woken up at night. "Aaaaaaaaooooo" the siren! Running down stairs! "Quick! Hurry up!" "Aaaaaaaarrrrrrrr"—the bombers! You could hear the drone, and out in the garden seeing the stars, you know, and "boom! boom! boom boom boom!" and seeing the searchlights ... "come on! get in the shelter!" ... mothers and grandmothers screaming at you ...*'

... After a while, of course you just stayed down there. Certain hours, you stayed there ... It was the Fruit Exchange for us, Spitalfields Market. Underneath it were huge catacombs which they converted into air-raid shelters. Each family had a set of bunks and there was a canteen down there and a rest-room and a ping-pong room ... And then up at seven in the morning, fires in the sky, hose pipes all over the road ... But best of all was the tubes. Did you ever sleep down there? We used to take long rides on the trains ...'

'... *exciting times for a child ... the whole business of war itself ... playing in and out of the bomb sites ... making houses out of bomb-rubble, used-up lace curtains, old boxes ... jagged walls to balance on, cellars to explore, ruins to play war games ...'cos I mean to say—who knew any better? ...*'

'... Remember the Bethnal Green tragedy, one day a siren, hundreds of people flocking down the stairs, and at the bottom someone stumbled ... Even those who knew what was happening couldn't do anything about it because they were being pushed ... three hundred killed ...'

Collection: Mr C. Ming

'... *Now? ... Well, neighbours are just curtain-merchants aren't they? Followed the pattern of the war. As the war years faded away the hardness set in ... People seemed to withdraw ... into theirselves, become more competitive. A change of quality come over the place, where people no longer brought chairs to sit out on the pavement, or sat on the stairs of a summer evening with the kids having picnics in front of their own doorstep ... started to disappear when I was about thirteen, or getting on for ... to deteriorate ...*'

Collection: Mr T. H. Templeman

'... Jewish Infants School ... Commercial Street Elementary ... Christ Church ... great Victorian blocks weren't they? with large rooms for air and huge windows to let the light in ... Upton House Central ... that wasn't a very good school but there was an English master ... gave me high marks for my compositions and turned a blind eye to bad spelling, bad grammar and a total indifference to the set theme ... I was expelled once ... we had this schoolmistress, used to sit on the top of a vacant desk with her legs open, and she took us for typing. We used to have to do typing after normal school hours and I was good at it and one evening didn't feel like staying behind. "I've got to have my hair cut, miss," I told her. "Where's your note?" she asked. "I'll bring one tomorrow," I told her. "You'll sit down and work," she replied. "I'm going!" "You'll stay!" "I'm going!" "You'll stay!" Finally I just sat in the desk, defiant, and did no work. Next day the head stormed into the science lab. "Wesker! Pack your books and go." I stood up, walked the length of the lab, said nothing and walked past him. "You know what you can do," he said, "apologize or go!" "I'm going," I said and walked away, my knees trembling, really trembling, and my heart going boom! boom! boom! The next day a part-time master, Jewish, who used to take us for religious instruction, knocked at the door and tried to persuade my mother to send me back and apologize. "Look," he said, "after all, we're only guests in this country and sometimes it's necessary to eat humble pie ..." BANG! That did it! My mother was furious. Poor man, he'd chosen just the right person to say *that* to ...'

'... Our school had a race of bullies inside it ... certain class of people in the school would bully and terrorize the rest. A bit like public school, you know? In reverse! Very reverse! 'Cos ours was a very working-class school all right ... This group'd get everyone and put them in this big bin in the playground, full of orange-peel, you know, rubbish. And you'd get as many as a dozen kids crammed in this space—a coal bin, not much bigger than that desk ... you'd be in there like sardines and they'd keep you in there for hours, in the summer, and jump on you and that. We used to be in terror ... the "ceremony of being put in the bin," putting your head down the lavatory—that type of thing ... Never had any pride, never sort of got together for a little battle with another school. No comradeship. Strange sort of school ... Evil school ...'

Collection : Della and Ralph Saltiel

'... I'm trying to remember the name of the school that we always used to have snowball fights with, on the bombed site, across Homerton High Street, remember? Across the road from Upton House ...'

'It wasn't Berger Road?'

'It *was* Berger Road!'

'*My sister went there. Churchill Walk was only round the corner from Upton House ... Here! now here's a funny thing ... you know they always used to say that if the Berger paint factory went up in smoke then the whole of Hackney would burn with it, well, one day it* did *catch fire and my uncle Ken, who of course lived in Churchill Walk, number four, he panicked and started running and when he stopped he found himself miles away in the middle of Hackney Marshes! ... Yes, I remember that site ... a stick of bombs fell on it, wallop! wallop! wallop! ... under the railway arches ...*'

'... We had marvellous fights on it ... with Berger Road school ... I remember that every so often in the lunch hour, a kind of ritual it became, some kids would come into the playground and yell, "Berger Road are attacking! They've got some of our boys!" And the whole playground would go— whoosh! And it was great! There we were in crowds, and we'd rush to the defences and I'd organize them in a military style with front ranks throwing the snowballs and back ranks making them and bringing up supplies ... till it got rough and they started putting stones in them ...'

'*... Always ended like that didn't it? ... makes you sick ... But we had a good headmaster though, lots of nice modern ideas, you know ... We built our own stage and we put on plays ... One of the first schools to do it. He went to America, apparently, and saw lots of things there and he brought the ideas back ... But he had to fight the authorities. Do you know we even had a radio sound system in our school? Years before any other school had it. We used to do our own broadcasting, things like Bastille Day. The storming of the Bastille! I was in it once, in one of the crowd scenes, and I got chucked out for laughing ... That was nearly my one radio performance. I got the sack! Ha! Became a pastry-cook instead ...*'

Collection : Mr Stephen Schama

' ... But there were friends. Friends! I was *made* by my friends, they sharpened me, criticized me, encouraged me ... kept me on my toes ... Our flat in Weald Square was always the kind of place you could bring people for drinking tea and arguing politics and listening to the radio ... we got everything from the radio: concerts, plays, lectures ... I was educated by the family, my friends and the B.B.C., not by any old school ... '

'...You've got to understand this: my grandfather had a business where at one time he employed as many as twelve men, which in them days was quite a business, you know? And where my grandmother'd remember men knocking at the door for their wages, and my grandfather had gambled them away playing "pieman" and having asked them to come back tomorrow. Or at other times she'd see piles of sovereigns on the table for wages, right? And nothing for them to buy the kids to eat so he'd go away for three days shooting and come back and throw a couple of ducks on the table and say, "Cook them!" Wouldn't give an explanation where he'd been, no! Nothing... Politics in our house? Politics to him was—well, he just had nothing to do with them. I'd hear him moan about Hitler and that, but everyone moaned about Hitler didn't they?... So, anything wrong with the world was blamed firmly on my grandfather...'

Collection: Mr Brian Clemens

'...Putting in Springfield Park...rowing on the river Lea...open air swimming and boating in Victoria Park...indoor swimming in Hackney Baths...good friends...what was there to complain about?...'

'...*Here! do you associate sounds with anything? What sounds do you remember in Fashion Street? Whenever I hear the drip of water on something, metal usually, that takes me right back to Churchill Walk. Used to be a big tin bath hanging on the wall outside, and after it rained you used to hear this drip, drip on the tin bath outside in the yard...*'

'...Who *didn't* have tin baths! We'd heat water in the enamel basin, the kettle, the saucepan—anything—and put it on the table in front of the fire, at least for my bath we did...Same in my wife's house, in Norfolk, *they* had a tin bath right up till recently, farm labourer's cottage...in the evenings I'd have my bath in front of the fire, my mother-in-law every now and then filling up a sooty old kettle that she'd put among the coals, full of lovely soft rain water which they'd caught in the big tank outside. Loved it! But sounds? No...I don't think so...wait! yes! I'm just remembering... the sound of peeing into an enamel chamber pot...'

'...*the drip, drip, drip, on the tin bath for me...*'

'...I asked my mother what she could remember of Fashion Street. She said, "I don't *want* to remember. I don't think I'll ever remember anything about Fashion Street. Nowhere in my life have I regretted to live anywhere than in Fashion Street"...There's a preservation order on it now. Seems they were specially built for the Jewish immigrant tailors...so behind the houses they erected these long, narrow factories—sweat-shops we called them. Of "architectural importance" now...Only now they're filled with Pakistani women—and child labour, they say...'

'...*the drip, drip, drip, on the tin bath...that and the cracking of coke in the grate...*'

' ... I mean to say, I cried for weeks to my mother,
who as you know was a widow at that time, till
she saved up her pennies and bought a bicycle for me
off a man who used to make second-hand bikes up ...
best thing I ever had in me life ... went cycling to
Seaford and Brighton and places like that on it, on
this old bicycle ... And you know that's not sentimental,
that's the truth! It's bloody fact! ...'

Collection : Mr John Dashwood

'...First job I ever had was in the bake-house in
Churchill Walk. Ikey Silver! It was his place. Well
my mother told me it was my father's first job, too.
Amazing isn't it? That's Bill Allin, my real father,
not Fred Chapman, my step-father. And my mother,
she always used to tell this story of how one day my old
man left one of the oven cloths in the tin, the tin
where the loaf was, so it was in the loaf! And old
Ikey Silver chased him round and round the bakehouse
hitting him over the head with it, with this loaf, this
loaf with the cloth in it ...'

'...That makes three of us were pastry-cooks:
you, me and Ho Chi Minh! ...'

'...Me first job! A baker's lad! Learnt to ice cakes,
too. Trained as a pastry-cook but I got itchy feet.
Wanted to travel. So I give up pastry-making and
joined the navy ...'

'...Furniture-maker's apprentice...carpenter's
mate ... bookseller's assistant ... plumber's mate ...
We all had so many jobs before we knew what we
were... Not that I was ever *out* of work, always
worked, but I kept changing ... farm labourer ...
seed sorter ... kitchen porter ... pastry-cook ...'

'...Pastry-cook ... merchant seaman ... tree-cutter ...

parks attendant ... gentle things for me, I'm a coward, me, can't bear pain or watching others with it ... don't ever want to die! In fact I don't think I'll be buried, think I'll start a family tomb instead, where they put the coffins in the cellar without nailing them down so's you can get out if they've made a mistake, know what I mean ... ?'

'... Ach! It's obsessive, the past ... something wrong ... I keep thinking it saps your energy ... but hell! What can you do? Places, buildings, names— they *do* carve strong images ... Hackney Baths is where I used to go swimming and have my hot wash. Every Saturday morning! 1st class wash! That was an important function for Christ's sake!... "More hot, number 7, please!" Your voice made a distinct sound, sitting in this iron bath, filled with water, between four walls, in a small cubicle. And I'd lie back and listen to the conversations people used to have with each other while they were soaking ... "More hot coming up, number 7, mind your backs ... hurry along there please, time's up, number 7 ..." And then, "Number 7 out!" I enjoyed yelling that. Made me feel important, responsible ... distinct sounds ... My father used to be across the passage taking a "schwitz" in the Turkish baths ... he took me once ... I stayed in too long and slept all afternoon ...'

Collection: Mr and Mrs Eric Cass

'... What can I *do*? Hackney swimming pool is the place where my first watch was stolen ten days after I'd been given it as a barmitzvah present. Of *course* I'll remember it! All of it! Everything! Indulgent uncles, tender aunts, kind, passionate ... barricades at Gardner's Corner ... the whole family involved in stopping Mosley marching through the East End ... Jesus! I bet the cream of the local Left 'lived' in Fashion Street and my aunt's flat—Charlotte de Rothschild's Dwellings, number one three four! Full of pouffes and books! Of *course* I'll remember it! I got my first reads off my aunt's bookshelves ... Upton Sinclair ... Howard Fast ... Tolstoy ... Turgenev ... and didn't I used to play their records endlessly, *endlessly*! Heavy old 78's of Gigli singing *Tosca* and *La Bohème*, and sets of record-books—Menuhin playing Paganini, Kreisler playing Brahms ... I mean they weren't flush but they used to save up threepenny pieces in order to buy records and books ... Of course I'll remember it!'

'... I keep dreaming about the East End ... When they pulled down Rothschild's Dwellings I dreamt about them being built again but there was an orchestra in the playground, a big one, a philharmonic, and trees and us playing games ...'

Collection : Anne Cuneo

'... Well, of course, I'm still living in my area, you're not ... I'm still living in my past. The difference is that. Perhaps in years to come, when I move, when I'm out of it, of having people come and go and never being able to invite them properly to have a civilized meal or sit down and talk, maybe I'll have dreams ... but just now, well, my dreams are waking dreams ... of having somewhere ... of being able to move through rooms and invite people for the weekend, say "Come and stay and we can discuss this and that" ... but in an area of my choosing, which I'd like ... which is definitely not the East End, I mean, you know how I started painting don't you? In prison! Well, when I come out the kids at school give my kid a rough time ... narrow-minded lot they were round there. 'Course, the silly bloody journalists didn't help. "Jail-bird becomes painter!" You'd've thought I'd done God knows what ... I mean the neighbours used to say things like "Look at 'im! Jail-bird and he's on telly! Ought to be sent back inside the nick!" Yes, straight up! It wasn't easy ... everyone recognized me and used any opportunity to take the mickey ... I was the oddity in the district, the lazy fat bastard who paints ... You know what they say if you win the pools: you lose all your friends—those who don't come near because they think you think they're hanging around after your money, and those who are! ... Give me half a chance and I'd move, mate. To a small area. I'd love to have a boat, nothing too ambitious, in Folkestone or Brighton ... a boat ... And besides, what they've done with the East End is diabolical, diabolical! They've just scuppered it, built and built and torn down and torn out and took lots of identity away and just made it into a concrete nothing ...'

Collection: Mr Bill Staughton

'... But people go on, don't they? Eating their eels and giving their custom where they've always given their custom ... Funny how people go on and take everything and anything. 'Course sometimes it's a good thing but—I don't know—not to object sometimes and say "Woah! that's my house you're pulling down" ... where I come from the majority used to think they weren't allowed to object, they used to just want to be patted on the back ... I had an uncle, uncle Sid he was called, he used to be a lavatory attendant in those toilets back of the Hackney Empire. Remember those toilets there? And then the Empire was turned into a TV theatre and you used to get all sorts of personalities come in after that ... well, the proudest day my uncle had was when Lord Boothby came in and give him a shilling for keeping a clean toilet ... Proudest day of his life. Funny thing a family is ... the way they react to you being an artist ... I got this other uncle used to come and look at my paintings and say, "No! no! that's not how it goes, that's all wrong," and he'd take out his pencil: "Look!" he'd say, "I'll show you!" And he'd've gone all over my canvases if I'd've let him ...'

'... I've got an uncle who, when he was driven to the first night of my first play in London, got out of the car, looked up, saw my name in lights and wept ...'

Collection : Professor Monica Mannheimer

'...In 1967 I give up painting for a year. "Forget your aspirations of becoming a painter," I said. "Forget them! Those ambitions, forget them!" So I did ... stopped for a whole year. And then when I started again I thought I'd go abstract ... black holes in brown backgrounds symbolizing windows in brick-work! No framework and just Naples yellow for sun-light ... cut out all details ... simplify! ... Didn't last long, though, my abstract period, five paintings, did them on hardboard and destroyed most of them. I think one acquaintance has still got one ... put it on his radiator he did, but it fell behind so he left it there ... until I began being taken notice of, then it started creeping up the wall. I'm waiting for it to reach the living-room ... Yes, gave up abstract ... decided people were more important ...'